To my editor, Prossy

The author, the artists, the editor, and the art director wish to thank the following for their most kind and expert help in the making of this book: Mr. J. A. Dale, Public Relations Officer, Miss Joan Crammond, and Mr. Sam Morton, all of the Zoological Society of London, Regent's Park; Dr. Theodore Reed, director of the National Zoo, Washington, D.C., Mr. Larry Collins, National Zoo, and Mr. Curley Harper, Jr., Mr. M. K. Rowe, and Mr. David Bryan, all of the National Zoo; and to Miss Susan Pearson, and Mrs. Marjorie Laidman, M.B.E., both of London; Mrs. Beryl Harris of Bognor Regis, Sussex; and also from England Mrs. Michael Benton, Winchester, and Miss Joyce Winmill, Henham, Bishop's Stortford; Miss Dorothy Dean of New York, Mr. Arthur Neuhauser of *The New York Times,* Mr. Stephen Shore of New York; Mr. Teng Mo-ling, Washington, D.C.; Miss Laura Chou and Miss X. X. Cheung of the China Institute in America, New York; and Mrs. Charlene Gridley, Reston, Virginia, Mrs. Ruthanna Long, Larchmont, N.Y., and Miss Claudia Weill of New York.

The Giant Panda Book

by Anthony Hiss

pictures by Greg and Tim Hildebrandt

 Golden Press • New York

Western Publishing Company, Inc., Racine, Wisconsin

Copyright © 1973 by Western Publishing Company, Inc. Printed in the U.S.A.
Golden, A Golden Book® and Golden Press® are trademarks of Western Publishing Company, Inc.
Library of Congress Catalog Card Number: 73-78209

Second Printing, 1974

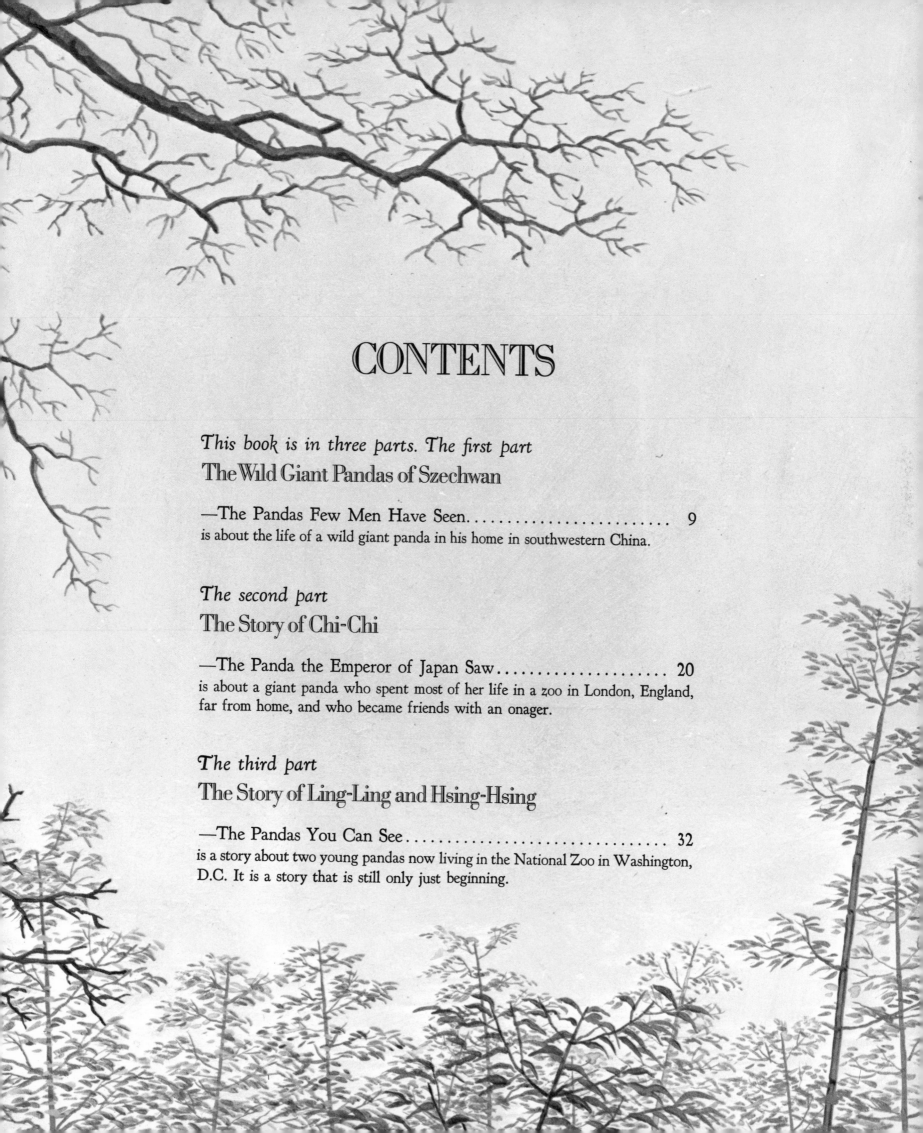

CONTENTS

The Wild Giant Pandas of Szechwan

THIS IS a wild giant panda sitting in his home, doing what the giant panda likes to do better than anything else in the world. He is eating a shoot of bamboo, about as big around as four of your fingers put together.

As soon as he finishes this shoot, he will bite off another one, and eat it, too. In fact, he will probably eat about fifteen to twenty shoots in this place, and then move on to another place nearby, where he will eat fifteen to twenty more shoots. He will go on eating almost all day (stopping every now and then and especially around noon for a nap, just for variety). Of course he eats bamboo leaves as well.

Bamboo is a kind of woody grass. It is a kind of grass that has been growing in the world much longer than the grass we know. It has a hollow jointed stem, and it can grow to a great height. There are many kinds of bamboo. The kind of bamboo the giant panda eats is bright green in color, like jade.

One reason he eats all day is that there isn't much nourishment in a single bamboo shoot. Another reason is that only the top part of each shoot is tender enough to eat, sort of like the vegetable asparagus. And the third reason, of course, is that he finds the taste so delicious.

You might think our wild giant panda would run out of food before very long. But he won't, because his home is a dense bamboo forest. (A bamboo forest is a forest that has a very few beech trees and hemlock trees and otherwise nothing but bamboo.) Everywhere he looks, endlessly, all he can see is his favorite food.

Where in the world can we find this panda and his bamboo forest?

There are, after all, several thousand giant pandas living somewhere in the world. There are two young giant pandas—named Ling-Ling and Hsing-Hsing—who live in Washington, D.C. And there are two slightly older pandas—Lan-Lan and Kang-Kang—who live in Tokyo. There are two slightly younger pandas—Yen-Yen and Li-Li—who live in Paris. And three other giant pandas live in Pyongyang, North Korea. But all these pandas live in zoos. So they cannot be the wild panda we are looking for.

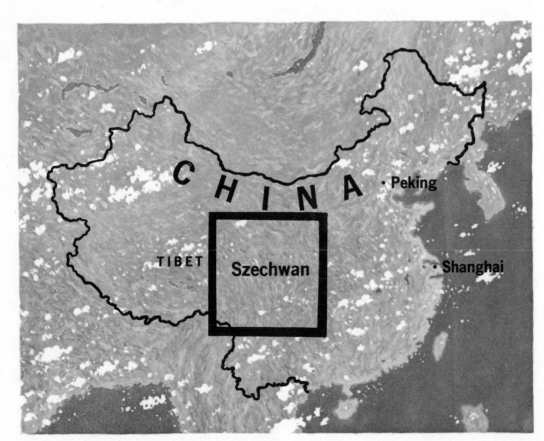

Every other panda in the world lives in China.

Eleven Chinese giant pandas live in Chinese zoos: five in the Peking Zoological Gardens, including a male cub caught in Szechwan in early 1973 by a hunter, three in the Shanghai Zoo, and one in each of these three cities: Nan-ching, Ha-erh-pin, and Hang-chou. So these aren't the panda we're after. All the rest of the Chinese giant pandas are wild and live within a large square area in the southwest of China and this area does have a number of forests in it.

A man once saw three pandas eating crocuses and tufts of grass on a meadow in Eastern Tibet, which is in this area.

But again, these were not our bamboo-eating pandas.

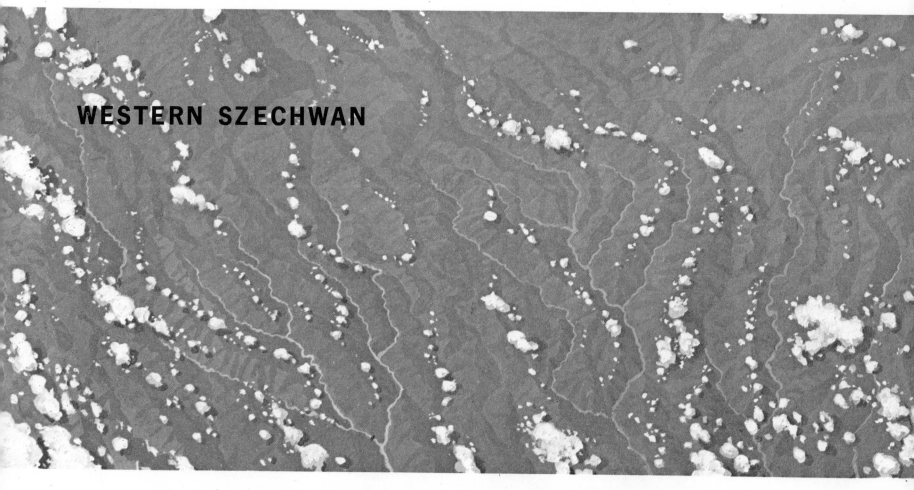

WESTERN SZECHWAN

Another man saw a panda on top of a mountain 13,000 feet high in Szechwan, where no trees grew. This couldn't be our panda, could it? He likes places that support bamboo forests.

A thousand feet below this peak was a rhododendron forest which stretched another 500 feet down the slope. Just beyond the rhododendron forest was—what? A bamboo forest. So, yes, the animal on the mountain top was our panda, out for a stroll.

All the areas in green in the map just above are mountainous bamboo forests in western Szechwan. This is where the wild Chinese giant pandas live.

The mountains of western Szechwan run north and south. They are very steep, and they are called the "Cut-Across" Mountains—Hengtuan—because they cut across China at this point and are hard to cross over. Most people in China live to the east of these mountains where the land is flatter and better for farming. And these farm people of the east don't pay much attention to the hill folk of western Szechwan or to their high country.

The hill folk themselves don't spend much time in the bamboo forests, because of the highness, the steepness, and the thickness. The forests are high up on the sides of the Cut-Across Mountains, and the mountain sides are very steep.

The bamboo in the forests grows so thickly that in many places people can only make their way through it on their hands and knees.

The only paths through the bamboo are the small trails made by the pandas. Even these trails, it is said, cannot be followed with ease by men, only by the mountain animals: leopards, black bears, takins, and wild pigs. (Takins look quite a lot like goats and also quite a lot like antelopes.)

The temperatures in the mountains are cool and cold. It snows in the winter, and there are heavy rains every May. The rest of the year the rains come and go, and when they leave they dry off very quickly. The air is very clean and comfortable. Sometimes, after it rains, snowy-white fingerlike mushrooms grow out of bamboo on the ground.

The mushrooms are very soft and very crunchy and very delicious. Baby pandas, who can't even bite bamboo shoots are particularly fond of them. Even grown-up pandas love eating these mushrooms almost as much as they love eating bamboo shoots. In the winter, when there aren't many bamboo shoots, you can sometimes see a panda walking slowly through the snow looking for them.

The hill folk live on the lower slopes, for the most part, where they farm and hunt. Every now and then, a panda will raid one of their farms, coming down out of the forests to steal a chicken or dig up a potato or swipe some honey from one of the farmer's beehives.

But very few of these hill folk — the people living closest to the giant pandas — have ever seen one. So you can see that hardly anyone in the world knows anything at all about pandas. When you have read all of this book, you will know more about them than all but the wisest of the hill folk.

The Chinese say they are sending people up into the mountains to get to know the pandas and to study them. The Chinese are proud that they live in the same country that the pandas live in, and they will not let anyone kill a panda. Perhaps they will have something new to tell us about pandas soon.

The Chinese word for the giant panda is *da-shung-mao* (these Chinese characters were on the pandas' crates sent to Washington) which means big-bear-cat. In Chinese it looks like this:

da   *shung*   *mao*

It takes five months for giant panda babies to be born. When a baby is born it weighs only five ounces, about the weight of a stick of butter. It is born with its eyes closed, and it has no teeth.

In 1963, a baby giant panda named Ming-Ming was born in the Peking Zoo. This was the first giant panda born in captivity. Ming-Ming's keepers reported that for the first month of his life his mother never let him out of her arms. During this time he opened his eyes for the first time. When he was two months old, his mother played with him by tossing him from arm to arm. Back and forth, back and forth, gently back and forth. If he got upset, she stroked his head. At two-and-a-half months he cut his first teeth. At three months he could walk.

Young giant pandas are very playful, as we shall see. It takes about three years for them to grow up.

When they are fully grown, they weigh about 300 pounds, which is about the weight of a big kitchen range. They measure about six feet, nose to tip of tail. Males are slightly bigger than females. Pandas are solid and heavy; they move slowly most of the time, and they play only a few minutes of the day.

They enjoy scratching themselves against hard objects. They sharpen their claws on tree trunks. They have 42 teeth.

They live by themselves, it is thought, but nobody is really sure. Their days are full of eating and sleeping and walking around their homes. Sometimes they climb trees.

They sleep in the forks of trees, underneath trees, inside hollow trees, or curled up in the bamboo of the bamboo forest. They sleep on their backs, on their sides and on their bellies. One panda once used the top of a tree stump for a bed.

Pandas walk on all fours. They can stand up on their hind legs without anything to support them, and reach for bamboo over their heads, but nobody has ever seen them walking on two legs.

Their feet turn in when they walk from place to place. In addition, they are bow-legged. On top of that, their arms and legs and their chests are heavy with big muscles. All of this makes their way of walking slow and deliberate and rolling and swaying, and rather uncomfortable looking.

The scientific name of the giant panda is *Ailuropoda melanoleuca.*
This means, in Latin, the-panda-footed-animal   that-is-black-and-white.
When scientists think up a name for an animal they look for things about that animal that make it different from all other animals.

When a naming scientist looks at a giant panda he sees only two things:

1) his front feet
2) his black and white coat.

Not many animals are only black and white, but they do exist. Zebras are black and white, and so are skunks. So *melanoleuca* (black and white) is only the second half of the panda's name.

No other animal has a front foot like a giant panda. So the scientists call the panda *Ailuropoda,* the-animal-with-the-panda-kind-of-front-foot. This means that if you see an animal, and you look at its front foot, and it has a front foot like a panda, then you must be looking at a panda. That is how scientists think.

Now, since the most important item in the life of a giant panda is bamboo, you might guess that his most unusual feature would have something to do with bamboo.

This is, in fact, true. The front foot of the giant panda is like a hand that is particularly good at picking up stalks of bamboo and holding them tight. It is sort of like a human hand, but with this difference. Instead of having four fingers and a thumb, the panda has five fingers and an extra-long wrist bone, which uses some of the muscles of the first finger. Moving the wrist bone and the five fingers, the panda can clamp his front foot tightly around a bamboo stalk— and even more tightly than he could if he had a hand that had only four fingers and a thumb.

Pandas sit up to eat. (Their tail is only five inches long and doesn't get in the way.) In order to chew bamboo, which is very tough, they have to have heavy heads, large jaws, thick jaw muscles, and big back teeth. It is hard for them to move their heads, except to chew. So the front foot keeps them alive by bringing the food to their head, and sticking it into the side of their mouth.

Here's how they eat: First they peel off the outer part of the bamboo by twisting their front feet from side to side while holding it tight with their teeth. Then they bite off a piece and chew it and eat it.

The giant panda is only a quarter the size of a horse, so the word "giant" is part of its name not because of its real size, but because of its size in relation to a smaller kind of panda called the red panda. The red panda also lives in western Szechwan, but since it doesn't eat just bamboo, it roams around a bit more, and lives in more places than the giant panda. The red panda is about the size of a fox. It is a beautiful animal with deep reddish fur and a long fluffy striped tail.

Everyone agrees that the giant panda and the red panda are closely related. Everyone also agrees that the *red* panda is related—a little more distantly—to the raccoon. So you might think that it was pretty obvious that the giant panda and the raccoon are members of the same animal family.

Are they? Well, in addition to scientists who think about what names animals should have, there are scientists who think about *where animals come from* and *where they belong* and *where they fit in* and things like that. These scientists, depending on where *they* come from, have different thoughts about what kind of animal the giant panda is and who its relations are.

American and English scientists, in general, think giant pandas and raccoons are related. But European scientists think, for the most part, that giant pandas belong in the bear family. They say that giant pandas are roughly the size of bears, and that giant pandas are very tiny when they are born, and so are bears. The Chinese have called pandas *big-bear-cats* for years. On the third hand, one American scientist at the University of California thinks of bears and pandas. He said in 1973 that panda blood is much more like bear blood than it is like raccoon blood.

On the fourth hand many bears hibernate, pandas don't. On the fifth hand, raccoon babies are tiny, like panda babies. And consider this: if you were a raccoon-sized panda, and one day you discovered how delicious bamboo was to eat, and you saw how much there was of it, and you started to eat and eat and get bigger (over the years), and if—at the same time—you had no natural enemies that could get through the bamboo to eat your babies (and pandas don't have natural enemies that can get through the bamboo to eat their babies), then maybe there wouldn't be any reason for your new-born babies to be bigger when first born.

I leave it to you to weigh these ideas, and think about them carefully, and decide just where giant pandas *do fit in*. You are now a scientist yourself.

The Story of Chi-Chi

This part of this book is a story—and a true story, too—about the life of one giant panda who left Szechwan and became, quite unexpectedly, a world traveler, famous throughout the planet, and the most famous animal in England. This panda's name was Chi-Chi, which means "naughty, mischievous little girl" in Chinese.

ONCE UPON A TIME (in November, 1956) Chi-Chi was born in the mountains of Szechwan. For six months she lived the life of an ordinary baby giant panda. She put on weight, and she cut her milk teeth (at the age of ten weeks). She learned how to eat bamboo, and how to play in the bamboo forest. If nothing else had happened to her, she would have spent her whole life right there, in Szechwan.

The following summer, on the 4th of July, some men came up into the mountains from the zoo in Peking. They were looking for a small panda to take with them back to that large city. The very first panda they saw was—Chi-Chi, of course. In less than a month, Chi-Chi was living in the Peking Zoo, eating bamboo and rice and fruit, and being looked after by a Chinese girl. If nothing else had happened to her, she would have spent the rest of her life right there, in the Peking Zoo.

20

The next spring, in May 1958, an animal dealer came to the Peking Zoo looking for a giant panda to take with him to an American zoo. There were no giant pandas in this country at that time, and there hadn't been any for five years. The Chinese had told the animal dealer that they would never sell a giant panda, but that it was possible they might swap. So the animal dealer brought with him to Peking three giraffes, two zebras, two rhinoceroses, and two hippopotamuses, and the Chinese agreed to take all these animals in exchange for one giant panda.

Now, let's look at those figures again. Out of them we can create what mathematicians call an equation. An equation gives you an idea of what something is worth by showing you what it is the same as. If someone asks you, "How much is a giant panda worth?" you can read that person the following equation: "1 giant panda = 3 giraffes + 2 zebras + 2 rhinoceroses + 2 hippopotamuses." ("=" means "equals," which is a word mathematicians use to mean "is the same as.")

The animal dealer was told he could pick any one of the three pandas in the Peking Zoo. He chose—Chi-Chi, of course. He put Chi-Chi in a special panda box, and flew off to Russia and to Germany, on his way to America. If nothing else had happened to her, she would have spent the rest of her life in a zoo in the United States.

But something else did happen, and what happened was this: something unexpected. Chi-Chi went to the London Zoo, in London, England, instead of coming to the United States. In those days, the United States government and the Chinese government were not good friends. Just at the time that Chi-Chi reached Germany, the United States government decided, unexpectedly, that not one thing that was Chinese could come to this country, even if that one thing was a small giant panda named Chi-Chi. So the animal dealer had to change his plans, and he sold Chi-Chi to the London Zoo. And that was the end of her travels, for the time being, at any rate.

The English were absolutely delighted to have an unexpected panda. They did everything they could think of to make her comfortable, and they also made her the most famous animal in the whole British Kingdom. This meant that she was even more famous than the special Welsh corgi dogs that belonged to the Queen, and even more famous than Goldie, the golden eagle, who also lives in the London Zoo. Goldie is famous for escaping twice from the Zoo. Chi-Chi escaped twice from *her* enclosure before she had been at the zoo a month. She didn't get very far —but of course she became even more famous. There were TV programs about her, and postcards of her, and photographs of her in the newspapers. People wrote books about her, and a Chinese restaurant in London changed its name to "Chi-Chi." Every day thousands of people came to look at her.

22

The London Zoo[1] built a special home for Chi-Chi, with an air-conditioned bedroom with two straw beds in it. One of the beds was close to the ground because, as we know, pandas like to sleep on the ground. The other bed was up some steps, about the height of a fork in a tree. We know that's another place pandas enjoy sleeping.

Chi-Chi was also given a large paddock to walk around and play in. The paddock had a number of toys to play with and a pool for wading. The Zoo even hired a sixteen-year-old keeper named Alan Kent just to play with her. That was in addition to her head keeper, Sam Morton, who looked after her and prepared her meals.

One of the things she ate was ten pounds of bamboo a day. Several people in different parts of England sent bamboo to the Zoo for Chi-Chi to eat, and the Polkerris Boy Scout Troop in Cornwall sent a lot of bamboo every day. People loved sending Chi-Chi bamboo, and sometimes they sent too much, but that was all right, because the elephants loved eating bamboo, too. So the Zoo just gave the extra bamboo to the elephants. Sam Morton also made a special dish for Chi-Chi every day called Panda Porridge. This was a very rich dish, and it had in it rice, dates, grapes, condensed milk, oranges, bananas, pears, and vitamins, among other things. You can see that the English knew a thing or two about how to make pandas happy.

And, as a matter of fact, for the next four years, Chi-Chi was very happy. She ate a lot and grew a lot and put on a lot of weight. In September 1958, when she arrived at the London Zoo, she weighed 122 pounds. Four years later she weighed almost twice as much. She had breakfast every morning at eight, and dinner in the middle of the afternoon. Between meals she slept and played games with Alan Kent. The pictures on this page show them playing three of her favorite games.

[1] This is what people who write books call a *footnote* about the word "zoo." The London Zoo is one of the biggest and oldest and most famous zoos in the world. It was originally called the London Zoological Gardens, because that is what all zoos were called. Then an Englishman named The Great Vance wrote a song about the London Zoological Gardens called "Walking in the Zoo is an O.K. thing to do." Everyone sang the song, and after that, everyone called the Zoo the Zoo. And that is where the word "zoo" comes from.

The next thing that happened to Chi-Chi was—she grew up. By the time she had been at the Zoo for four years she was a full-grown giant panda. She was five feet, six inches tall when she stood up on her hind feet, and that was as big as she was ever going to get. Now, a full-grown giant panda is not the same animal as a young giant panda. Grown-up pandas are not as interested in playing games as young pandas. And grown-up pandas are not quite as active as young pandas. The world is not so new for them, and they sleep later in the mornings.

The men who looked after Chi-Chi noticed these changes taking place in her without too much surprise. They knew that these things happen. But then they began to notice certain other changes. Several times a year, she stopped eating her Panda Porridge, and for a week or so would eat only tender bamboo shoots.

At these times she would run around her paddock barking— a noise completely unlike the noises she usually made, which were sort of bleating sounds. There were other times when she became bad-tempered, for the first times in her life. One day she bit a young keeper in the leg.

These changes in Chi-Chi disturbed the men who looked after her. It was obvious to them that she was no longer a happy panda. They spent a lot of time thinking about Chi-Chi and her unhappiness.

They were trying to think if there was anything they could do to make her feel better. Maybe she was lonely for another panda. Or maybe she wanted to have babies of her own. Were there any other pandas she could meet?

There was one, and that was An-An. An-An lived in the Moscow Zoo, and he was the only other giant panda in the world living outside of China at that time. An-An was a male panda, a year younger than Chi-Chi. Among other things, he lived on birch tree twigs and aspen tree twigs, because bamboo doesn't grow in Russia. He also drank Russian tea. He weighed 339 pounds, and he was really rather fat. He liked to sleep on his back with his legs resting on a log. When he slept like this he covered his eyes with his left fore-leg, and he snored. He was good-tempered.

The men at the London Zoo wrote the men at the Moscow Zoo suggesting a meeting between Chi-Chi and An-An. It took a long time—several years, in fact—to arrange anything. Finally, Chi-Chi was invited to Moscow. She was put in another special panda box, and in in the spring of 1966, she and Sam Morton, her head keeper, flew off to Moscow in a specially converted British European Airways Vanguard plane from which some of the seats had been removed. Sam Morton gave her a chocolate bar so she wouldn't feel nervous.

In Moscow, Chi-Chi was put in a cage next to An-An. They were immediately curious about each other, but when they were put together, they did not make friends. In fact, they snarled at each other. After that they were kept separate all summer. One day in October they were put together again. That day, the zoo closed early, and a special squad of policemen holding water hoses lined up outside their cage, in case they started to fight. Well, they didn't fight, but they didn't make friends either. Every time An-An got close to Chi-Chi, she barked at him and cuffed him with her paws. The same thing happened seven other days. So, the men in charge gave up, and Chi-Chi and Sam Morton flew home.

Two years later An-An came to London in a Russian plane. Chi-Chi was moved into a new home, with an even larger grass paddock that had lovely yellow wildflowers growing in it. But her new home didn't make her like An-An any better, and they never became friends. Sam Morton said, "An-An behaved like a perfect gentleman," and he liked An-An. But Chi-Chi never did. So An-An flew home.

And Chi-Chi was still unhappy. If nothing else had happened to her, she might never have been happy again for the rest of her life.

While he was in London, An-An had lived next door to Chi-Chi's new home in a large grassy paddock of his own. After An-An left London this paddock was empty. For about a year, Chi-Chi's life went on as it had before: rather dull except for all the visitors. Meanwhile, the grass in the paddock next door grew taller and taller.

Then one day, when Chi-Chi woke up late in the morning, there was another animal living in the grassy paddock next to hers. This animal was Leslie, and he was an onager, or wild ass. Onagers belong to the horse family, and the people in charge of the zoo had moved Leslie in next door to Chi-Chi because they wanted him to eat the grass and keep it trim. Horses love to eat grass, you know.

Leslie had been living at the London Zoo since November 1962, the month in which he had come to the zoo from northwest Persia, in Central Asia. Onagers are fast-running animals, and they live wild in herds on the plains of Central Asia. They look rather like wild donkeys. The Persian word for onager is *gur*.

Leslie stood about four feet high at the shoulders. He was a beautiful animal. His coat had short hair, and it was a sort of pinkish tan that was a little bit tawny and a little bit cream-colored. His mane was chocolate brown, and he had a narrow chocolate brown stripe along his spine, and tufts of black in his tail and in the tips of his ears. He lifted up his ears every now and then, and when he did you could see that they were very long, like a donkey's. He also had beautiful almond-shaped eyes.

In addition to the grass in his paddock, Leslie ate four to five pounds of carrots a day, ten pounds of clover or hay, a half bucket of oats and flaked maize (which is the English word for corn), an oil cake made of linseed oil and protein, and half a bundle of lucerne (which is the English word for alfalfa).

Oh, yes, I forgot to mention that Leslie's scientific name was *asinus equus onager,* which means wild-ass-horse-onager.

Now, you would hardly think that having Leslie for a neighbor would mean anything to Chi-Chi. Well, now, would you? Onagers and giant pandas live in different parts of the world, so they couldn't have much in common. And Chi-Chi was not used to the company of other animals. In fact, except for a lot of human beings, Chi-Chi had only known very few other animals in her thirteen years—her mother, a couple of other pandas, and a mallard duck and her ducklings that hatched out in her enclosure, two springs running.

As it happened, Chi-Chi paid no attention to Leslie at all for a week after his arrival next door. And then, quite suddenly, she began to take an interest in him. And at the same time, also quite suddenly, he began to take an interest in her. Within a month they had become dear, dear, close friends, and Chi-Chi was a happy panda once more.

The people in charge of the London Zoo had not expected Chi-Chi and Leslie to make friends, and when it happened they didn't know what to think. "We are puzzled by this strange relationship," said the people in charge.

The newspapers heard about it, and they sent photographers to take pictures of Chi-Chi and Leslie, and reporters to write stories about the friendship. The reporters didn't know what to make of it all, either. They were as confused as the people in charge. One newspaper ran a story about Chi-Chi and Leslie under a headline that said:

PAUL INTERESTS CHI-CHI,
BUT PAUL ISN'T A PANDA

They thought Leslie's name was Paul, which shows how confused they were.

Chi-Chi and Leslie continued to enjoy each other's company. Chi-Chi was by now an old panda. She slept until noon every morning. Leslie, who was younger, got up earlier, and he would spend the mornings waiting for Chi-Chi to wake up. He would pace along the fence between their two paddocks—down and up, up and down, down and up—looking all the time at the door to her bedroom.

28

Leslie had a tree stump in his paddock. Whenever he got tired of pacing up and down, he would rest his head on the tree stump and gaze at Chi-Chi's door.

Every now and then he would chase a flock of sparrows, just for exercise.

About noon Chi-Chi would emerge from behind her door. She walked slowly to the middle of her paddock where there was a clump of bushes. She broke off a branch of one of the bushes with her strong front paw, and then walked over to the fence where Leslie was waiting. Sitting up on her hind legs, she waved the branch back and forth in front of Leslie, and he leaned forward and chomped on the leaves as they swished back and forth in front of his face. This was the game they played every day.

Taking a branch over to Leslie was the first conscious act performed by Chi-Chi in the morning, so she must have had him on her mind when she woke up. He was good to her because he waited for her endlessly, and she was good to him because she would go over to him immediately, as soon as she got up.

CHI - CHI MAKES

Chi-Chi the giant panda, the most famous animal in the British Isles, made Hirohito the Emperor of Japan smile here yesterday, it was revealed.

Usually reliable sources close to the Emperor confirmed eyewitness sightings of the smile and discounted earlier rumors that the Emperor had frowned.

The sources suggested that these rumors emanated from people who had been standing on their heads.

(continued on page 10)

Sam Morton, Chi-Chi, Smiling Emperor Hirohito, seen here left to right

If you had been visiting London in October 1971, you would have seen lots of stories in the newspapers about Emperor Hirohito, the Emperor of Japan. The Emperor and his wife, Empress Nagako, were spending three days in London that month, and the English were quite excited because it was the first time that an Emperor of Japan and an Empress of Japan had ever come to see them.

The English did everything they could think of to make the Emperor feel at home. The Queen of England met him at the railroad station in her carriage. She gave him a great banquet in the white-and-gold state ballroom in her palace. The Lord Mayor of London gave the Emperor another

MPEROR SMILE !

banquet, and he was also taken on trips to famous places.

The English hoped the Emperor was having a good time. They knew how much they themselves enjoyed banquets and carriage rides and seeing famous places, but they couldn't tell whether the Emperor enjoyed them because the Emperor was a very dignified old man, and he did not smile very often.

On the last morning of their visit to London, Emperor Hirohito and Empress Nagako went to the London Zoo. They wanted to see Chi-Chi, because in all their years as Emperor and Empress they had never seen a giant panda. Now, Chi-Chi at this time was a very old lady, and she never got up before noon, not even to see Leslie. But that morning Sam Morton brought her a special breakfast of chocolate bars and bamboo shoots, and another keeper waved a broom, so that she could see that they were serious. She got up, and came outside, and there was the Emperor, and he was looking right at her, and he was smiling.

The next day the newspapers reported that the Emperor smiled *three times* at Chi-Chi. So the English knew that he had enjoyed himself after all, thanks to their beloved giant panda.

The Story of Ling-Ling and Hsing-Hsing

The rest of this book is about Ling-Ling and Hsing-Hsing. Ling-Ling and Hsing-Hsing are two young giant pandas who live in the National Zoo in Washington, D.C. They are the only giant pandas living in the United States. They are, with the two in Paris, the only giant pandas living anywhere in the western world, because both Chi-Chi and fat old An-An have come to the end of their days.

Ling-Ling means "cute little girl." She was born in Szechwan in October 1970, and if you feel like writing her name in Chinese, here is what it looks like:

玲 玲

Ling-ling

Hsing-Hsing is pronounced "Shing-Shing." Hsing-Hsing is a male giant panda who was born in Szechwan in April 1971. His name is written this way in Chinese:

新 新

Hsing-hsing

It means "new."

Ling-Ling and Hsing-Hsing are the biggest attractions in Washington. More people go to see them than to see the Capitol building (the building where Congress meets), or the Washington Monument, or even the White House. Sometimes as many as a thousand people come to see them in one hour.

Of course, like all pandas, Ling-Ling and Hsing-Hsing spend a great deal of their time sleeping, so that is all that most of their visitors ever see them do. But even watching them sleep can be interesting, because, like all pandas, Ling-Ling and Hsing-Hsing are always doing interesting things. When I went to see them, I saw them sleeping in positions I had never read about in any book, and if you have a chance to go see them yourself, you will probably see them sleeping in positions you have not read about in this book.

If you want to make sure to see them when they are awake, the best times to get to the Panda House are from about 9 until 11:30 in the morning, and from about 3:30 until 4:30 in the afternoon. They are fed every day at 9:30 A.M. and at 4 P.M. On cool days they go outside most mornings, from about 9 to 11, and then they have breakfast outdoors. But you would have to check with the Zoo to make sure just which days they will be going outside.

The story of how Ling-Ling and Hsing-Hsing came to the United States is a story made up of three events. The first event was that the President of the United States and his wife went to China. The second event was that two musk oxen, whose names were Milton and Matilda, also went to China. The third event was that Ling-Ling and Hsing-Hsing came from China to the United States.

A musk ox is a big, shaggy, gray-brown animal that lives in North America and has horns. It is something like an ox and something like a sheep. Milton and Matilda, the two musk oxen in our story, lived in the San Francisco Zoo before they went to China.

The President, President Nixon, went to China in February 1972. The time had come for the government of China and the government of the United States to begin to become friends, so the Chinese invited President Nixon and Mrs. Nixon to come visit them. When the President got to China he told the Chinese that he was going to send them a present. The present was going to be Milton and Matilda, the two musk oxen.

The Chinese were delighted to hear about their present, and they told the President that they would send two giant pandas at the Peking Zoo to the United States as their present to us. There were five giant pandas at the Peking Zoo at that time, and Mrs. Nixon went to see them all. Two of the five were — Ling-Ling and Hsing-Hsing, of course. The other three were a couple of twenty-year-old pandas, Li-Li and her husband Pi-Pi, and a small cub who had just been caught in Szechwan. All five pandas were in excellent health.

The Peking Zoo is a great zoo and very clean, and has many Chinese animals not found in other zoos — animals like the golden langur, two different kinds of takins, tufted deer, white-lipped deer, and Chinese macaques. Langurs and macaques are monkeys. Five million people visit the Peking Zoo every year, and it costs 2½¢ to get in.

The Chinese Prime Minister, Mr. Chou En-lai, said to Mrs. Nixon at a banquet: "You've given us oxen. We'll load up the plane with pandas."

Now the President had to make an important decision. He had to decide at which American zoo the pandas would live. There are many great zoos in this country, and of course each zoo hoped it would be chosen. The zoos were all particularly excited because there hadn't been any giant pandas in this country for twenty years.

The President knew that when he chose one zoo all the other zoos would be disappointed. He thought it over. Then he chose the National Zoo in Washington. He knew that this way nobody would be too disappointed, because Washington is our capital and therefore the only city that really belongs to everybody. Presidents like to make decisions that disappoint people as little as possible.

The National Zoo is one of the great zoos of the country. In addition to pandas, it has a number of other rare animals: four red pandas— father, mother, and two young ones; white tigers; coconut crabs; Patrick, the first baby Indian rhinoceros born in the United States; and a komodo dragon, the world's largest living lizard.

The President asked Dr. Theodore Reed, the director of the
National Zoo, to take Milton and Matilda to Peking and to bring
Ling-Ling and Hsing-Hsing home. Dr. Reed flew to China in an Air
Force jet cargo plane. The commander of the cargo plane was Major
Robert D. Mease. The freighter carried a crew of eleven.

Ling-Ling and Hsing-Hsing were put on board the plane on April 14th.
They were not at all frightened at being on board an airplane, because the
Chinese had already taken them on several plane rides in order to prepare
them for their flight to America.

Four Chinese came with the giant pandas to this country: a zoologist, a
head keeper, an interpreter, and a government man. The head panda
keeper's name was Mr. Yang.

The distance from Peking to Washington is ten thousand miles.
The plane's first stop was Guam, where Dr. Reed cut some fresh
bamboo for the pandas. On April 15th the plane stopped in Honolulu in
Hawaii. Early in the morning of April 16th the plane landed at Andrews
Air Force Base in Maryland, near Washington.

Security precautions at the airport were extremely tight. Air Force policemen were on patrol. Newspaper reporters were kept at some distance from the plane, and could see only the special panda boxes that had Ling-Ling and Hsing-Hsing inside. They weren't allowed to see the pandas. The boxes were put into trucks, and the trucks, escorted by police cars, rushed to the National Zoo. That was the pandas' introduction to the United States.

A few days later, Dr. Reed held a press conference. He said that both giant pandas were in good health. He said Ling-Ling weighed 136 pounds, and Hsing-Hsing weighed 74 pounds. He said Milton had a cold. He said, "You like musk oxen, but pandas can steal your heart away."

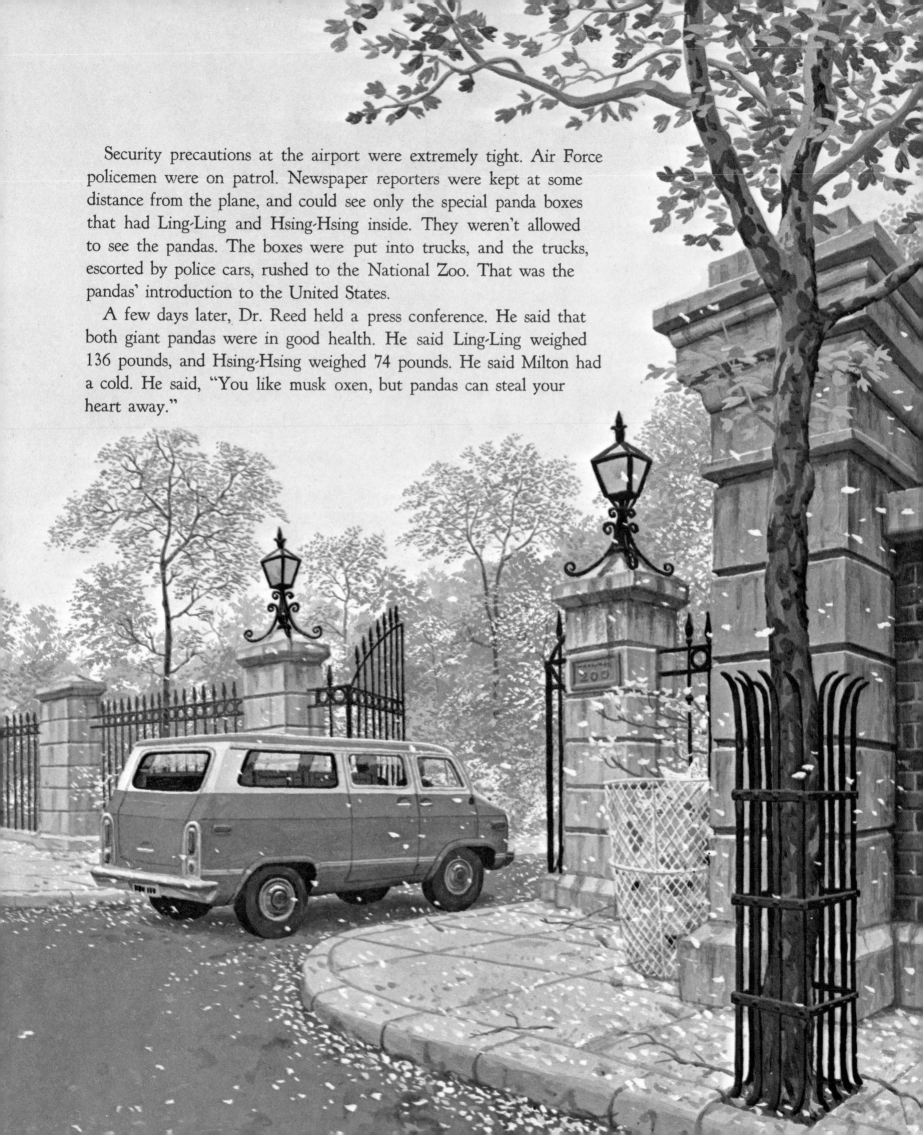

Ling-Ling and Hsing-Hsing live next door to each other in a special Panda House. They are being kept separate, for the time being, and only see each other when they are allowed outside. The man in charge of the Panda House is Larry R. Collins. As soon as Larry R. Collins was given this job, he flew to England and talked to Sam Morton. Sam Morton told him everything he knew about pandas. There are also three keepers in the Panda House: Curley Harper, Jr., M. K. "Tex" Rowe, and David Bryan. All three of them were specially chosen to look after the giant pandas because of their good work with other animals at the zoo. They wear special uniforms with shoulder patches that say "PANDA UNIT."

Curley Harper, Jr. says: "The Chinese sent us a beautiful pair of animals. We are not trying to tame them. We respect their right to be wild animals. I'm responsible for those animals. They can't get their own food here in the zoo, so I'm going to give them the best care I can. It is quite an honor to work with the two most important animals in the Western Hemisphere."

Ling-Ling and Hsing-Hsing each have a large air-conditioned cage (temperature: 50° Fahrenheit), a small private sleeping den, and a big back yard. (The fences around the yards have had to be raised because the young giant pandas have been getting so much bigger.) Each large cage has a big log pile for sleeping or climbing or just lying around on top of, tubs of bamboo for snacks, and a big white plastic ball to play with.

Ling-Ling, who is very playful, is also very intelligent. She took one of the tubs of bamboo and converted it into a toy. She dug out the

plants, and began to roll the tub around, and to attack it, and to bite it. She also tries to solve problems. When she was playing outside one day, she saw some bamboo in Hsing-Hsing's yard and decided to get it. There was a beer keg in her yard, so first she pushed it up against the fence in between the two yards and tried to climb over. After that, she tried to dig her way under the fence.

Hsing-Hsing is much quieter than Ling-Ling. He sleeps more, and, in his first months, in Washington, didn't play much at all. Now he plays more. He spends a lot of time in his little den. The keepers call him "Junior." They call Ling-Ling "Clown." Both animals know their names.

When they are playing outside they turn front somersaults, and cartwheels on their sides. Their eyesight is not the greatest. They can see about 8 feet in front of them. Their senses of hearing and smell are very powerful.

Besides bamboo, they eat rice, vitamin drops, bone meal, salt, honey, cat food, apples, carrots, kale, sweet potatoes, cantaloupes, and milk-bone dog biscuits. They also eat grass. It costs about $4000 a year to feed the pandas. The Zoo says that's only $1000 less than it costs to feed

4 elephants for a year. Larry R. Collins says that Hsing-Hsing would sell his soul for a slice of bread and honey.

They each have two toys outside: a metal beer keg and an orange-yellow-and-blue plastic ball. The beer kegs were given to them by a man who owns a bar near the Zoo. They both like to try to climb on top of their balls: Ling-Ling is better at it than Hsing-Hsing. She can actually balance herself on top of the ball without falling off.

Each yard also has some small bamboo trees. One of Ling-Ling's favorite games is pulling the bamboo trees over on top of herself, and chewing on the leaves.

Their favorite game is rolling around. Ling-Ling likes to roll on her back, put her left front paw over her nose, and then just roll sideways, over and over. Hsing-Hsing likes to roll on his back, bite his tail and hold on to it, and then just roll backwards, over and over. He also likes to stand on his head in front of the fence near Ling-Ling. Sometimes they roll the length of their yards together, one on each side of the fence.

41

The food is prepared in a room at one end of the Panda House. This room is also the place where the records of each panda are kept. The keepers weigh the pandas about the 27th of each month, an important part of the panda records. On February 27th, 1974, Hsing-Hsing weighed 269 pounds and Ling-Ling weighed 264 pounds. There is a log book for each panda, in which the keepers write down every day what the animal has done. There is a folder of notes about what to do. Tex Rowe has drawn several panda heads on its cover. Out back, is a motor scooter for the keepers to use. It is called "THE BAMBOO EXPRESS."

The day I visited the Panda House I had a chance to watch both pandas for some time. First I saw them eating breakfast. Hsing-Hsing was the more interesting eater. Breakfast was served in a pan placed on the floor. Hsing-Hsing sat down in front of his pan, and stuck his muzzle into it in order to eat all the soft food first. First he ate all the rice. Then he used his right front paw to break up the cat food, which was a little lumpy, and to pull it towards his mouth. He is a serious and thorough eater. Then he took his sweet potato and took it into his sleeping den. He sat down. He held it first in his left front paw and then in his right. Then he stuck it into the back of his jaw and chewed on it like a lamb chop. He dropped a piece and picked it up with one of his back feet. Then he stood up on all fours and shook his head in order to wipe his mouth, and sat down again. When he sat down, he stuck his left back foot straight up into the air and leaned his left forearm on it. He could also scratch his chin with the claws on his back feet.

Later I saw him walking around with a carrot in his mouth. The carrot was sticking straight out the front of his mouth.

He chewed each mouthful at least six times before swallowing.

Ling-Ling was the more interesting sleeper.
She slept on the log pile. First she slept on her tummy
with her legs straight out, imitating a rug.

Then she rolled over on her right side, and brought her left front paw
up over her eyes, like a kitten. Then she rolled over on her back and stuck
her tongue out. Then she yawned and scratched her muzzle with her left
hind foot. Then she yawned again and stretched all four legs. Then she
put both front paws over her eyes. Then she scratched her tail with her
right back foot. Then she rolled over on her left side and pushed both
front paws down between her hind feet. Then she scratched her right
front paw with her right back foot. Then she stuck her tongue out again.
Then she rolled over some more so that she was back on her tummy
again. This time her right hind foot was sticking straight *down*.

If you ever do go to see Ling-Ling and Hsing-Hsing, you might want to talk to them. Here are some Chinese phrases you could use if you wished.

chr fan	eat rice
chao an	good morning
wan an	good night
gwai gwai	be good
hau buhau?	how are you?
bao bubao?	are you full?
Ling-Ling haukan	pretty Ling-Ling
Hsing-Hsing haukan	pretty Hsing-Hsing